PRESENTED TO:

_____

Life is fragile—
handle with prayer.

Author Unknown

PRESENTED BY:

_____

Life's Daily Prayer Book for Fathers
© 2005 Elm Hill Books
ISBN: 1-404-18518-6

The quoted ideas expressed in this book (but not scripture verses)
are not, in all cases, exact quotations, as some have been edited for
clarity and brevity. In all cases, the author has attempted to maintain
the speaker's original intent. In some cases, quoted material for this
book was obtained from secondary sources, primarily print media.
While every effort was made to ensure the accuracy of these
sources, the accuracy cannot be guaranteed. For additions, deletions,
corrections or clarifications in future editions of this text, please
write ELM HILL BOOKS.

This manuscript written and compiled by Robin Schmitt in association
with Snapdragon Editorial Group, Inc.

Design and layout of cover and interior pages was created
by D/SR Design, LLC.

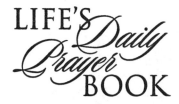

LIFE'S *Daily* *Prayer* BOOK

for Fathers

Prayers to Encourage and Comfort the Soul

Elm Hill Books
An Imprint of J. Countryman®

An old hymn goes: "What a friend we have in Jesus, all our sins and griefs to bear. What a privilege to carry everything to God in prayer." They're wonderful words, aren't they—comforting, strengthening, liberating. And they are words of truth! In the Bible, God invites us to friendship with Him, a friendship that urges us to cast all our cares on Him. Have you ever thought about talking to God as you would to a friend?

Life's Daily Prayer Book for Fathers was designed to guide and inspire you as you reach out to God in friendship and converse with Him concerning the issues, activities, and relationships that impact you as a father. Think of these written prayers as letters to your best friend—God. Make them your own by adding the names of family and friends and specific needs. And don't forget to record and date your answers. God bless you as you embark on this exciting spiritual adventure.

Life's Daily Prayer Book for Fathers
Prayers to Encourage and Comfort the Soul

Daily Prayers for . . .

Daily Prayers for Help . . .

To pray is to sit
open-handed before God.

Peter G. van Breeman

Daily Prayers…

Daily prayer for . . .
salvation

The gospel of Christ ... is the power of God
to salvation for everyone who believes.
Romans 1:16

Dear Heavenly Father,

When I was younger, I felt immortal. I don't feel that way anymore. Some guys may be able to keep pretending they'll live forever, but I've got to face reality. I know that someday my life will end. And when it does, I want to be with You for eternity!

Until then, I want to be the person—the man, the husband, the father—You created me to be. Someone You can count on to make good choices for my family. Someone who is a worthy role model for my children. I simply can't do that without Your help.

I need You, Lord, for now and forever. I give You my heart. Come in and be my Lord and Savior.

Amen.

Anyone who calls on the name of the Lord will be saved.
Romans 10:13 NLT

MY PERSONAL PRAYER

*It is not your hold of Christ that
saves you, but his hold of you!*
Charles Haddon Spurgeon

Dear Father:

_____

_____

_____

_____

_____

_____

Amen

*There's nothing like the written Word of God for showing you
the way to salvation through faith in Christ Jesus.*
2 Timothy 3:15 MSG

He who believes in the Son has everlasting life.
John 3:36

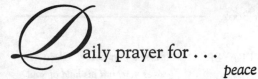

Daily prayer for . . .

peace

His name will be called Wonderful,
Counselor, Mighty God, Everlasting Father,
Prince of Peace.

Isaiah 9:6

Dear Heavenly Father,

My home has changed so much since my children were born. Before they came along, everything was orderly and calm. Home used to be a place where I could unwind after a stressful week at work. Now there are times when I want to head back to the office to escape the chaos!

What bothers me most is when my kids fight. I want our home to be a place of love and peace, a reflection of Your kingdom.

Help me to be like Jesus, whose trust in You gave Him such strong inner peace that He could rest during a storm. And when my little "disciples" start arguing among themselves, help me to be a peacemaker like Christ.

Amen.

Jesus said, "Peace I leave with you, My peace I give to you."
John 14:27

MY PERSONAL PRAYER

*Finding God, you have no need
to seek peace, for he himself is
your peace.*

Frances J. Roberts

Dear Father:

_____

_____

_____

_____

_____

_____

Amen

The Lord will bless His people with peace.
Psalm 29:11

*Glory to God in the highest,
and on earth peace, goodwill toward men!*
Luke 2:14

_D_aily prayer for . . .
wisdom

Teach us to make the most of our time,
so that we may grow in wisdom.

Psalm 90:12 NLT

Dear Heavenly Father,

Parenthood is one of the highest callings in my life, and I want to rise to this challenge. Yet I don't feel equipped for the job. When I became a dad, I suddenly realized I hadn't been trained for this! Sometimes I think when You chose me to be a father, You were looking at the wrong resume.

You've promised to give Your wisdom to anyone who asks for it. Please teach me how to raise these precious children You've entrusted to me. Speak to me through Your Word, through other Christians' advice, and by Your Spirit through prayer.

Help me to follow my earthly father's example, where it was godly and good. Most of all, help me to emulate You.

Amen.

The fear of the Lord is the beginning of wisdom; a good understanding
have all those who do His commandments.

Psalm 111:10

MY PERSONAL PRAYER

Knowledge is horizontal.
Wisdom is vertical—it comes
down from above.

Billy Graham

Dear Father:

_____

_____

_____

_____

_____

_____

Amen

How much better to get wisdom than gold! And to get
understanding is to be chosen rather than silver.
Proverbs 16:16

You desire honesty from the heart, so you can teach
me to be wise in my inmost being.
Psalm 51:6 NLT

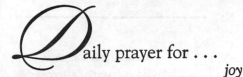

Daily prayer for . . .
joy

In Your presence is fullness of joy; at Your
right hand are pleasures forevermore.

Psalm 16:11

Dear Heavenly Father,

Children are such a blessing, and they really have
brought a lot of joy into my life. At the same time, the
stresses of parenthood constantly threaten to rob me of
that joy. Please help me not to allow this. When my
children look at me, I want my face to reflect the joy
I've found in being their father—and in knowing You.

The longer I walk with You, the more I understand the
difference between happiness and joy. I see now that true
joy, rooted in You, is much stronger than momentary
happiness; it can endure life's ups and downs. Help me
teach my children this truth. More importantly, help me
model it to them.

Amen.

Believing, you rejoice with joy inexpressible and full of glory.
1 Peter 1:8

MY PERSONAL PRAYER

*Joy is the great note
all through the Bible.*
Oswald Chambers

Dear Father:

_____

_____

_____

_____

_____

_____

Amen

*You have given me greater joy than those who
have abundant harvests of grain and wine.*
Psalm 4:7 NLT

*Jesus said, "These things I have spoken to you, that My joy
may remain in you, and that your joy may be full."*
John 15:11

*D*aily prayer for . . .
encouragement

> *O Lord, you will hear the desire of the meek;*
> *you will strengthen their heart.*
>
> Psalm 10:17 NRSV

Dear Heavenly Father,

As a dad, I need Your encouragement. I need to hear Your still, small voice telling me I'm doing okay. When I'm not doing so well, I need You to correct me too. But even then, Lord—especially then—I need Your affirmation.

In the same way, I know my children need my voice of approval. They thrive on my applause; I see it in their eyes. Please help me show my appreciation for their efforts and accomplishments more than my criticism for their mistakes. When I need to admonish them, help me do it lovingly and gracefully. I want to build them up, not tear them down. I want to encourage them the way You encourage me.

Amen.

> *May Jesus himself and God our Father,*
> *who reached out in love and surprised you with gifts*
> *of unending help and confidence, put a fresh heart in you.*
> 2 Thessalonians 2:16–17 MSG

MY PERSONAL PRAYER

Correction does much,
but encouragement does more.
Johann Wolfgang von Goethe

Dear Father:

_____

_____

_____

_____

_____

_____

Amen

Such things were written in the Scriptures
long ago to teach us. They give us hope and encouragement.
Romans 15:4 NLT

Be of good courage, and He shall strengthen your heart,
all you who hope in the Lord.
Psalm 31:24

Prayers to Encourage and Comfort the Soul   19

$\mathcal{D}$aily prayer for . . .

power

Be strong in the Lord and
in the power of His might.

Ephesians 6:10

Dear Heavenly Father,

Life as a parent is exhausting! Between earning a
living, maintaining the house, and caring for the kids,
sometimes I don't think I have enough energy to make
it through the day. It helps to know I can draw
strength from You, Lord. Help me remember to call on
You when I'm weary.

However, there's another type of strength I need even
more—the power of a godly father to influence his
children and the generations to follow. Fill me with
Your Spirit every day, because it's Your power within
me that will enable me to beat temptation and live
right. Give me the strength of character that only You
can provide, so my family will reap all Your blessings.

Amen.

I can do all things through Christ who strengthens me.
Philippians 4:13

MY PERSONAL PRAYER

When a man has no strength,
if he leans on God,
he becomes powerful.
Dwight Lyman Moody

Dear Father:

_____

_____

_____

_____

_____

_____

Amen

It is God who arms me with strength,
and makes my way perfect.
Psalm 18:32

God has not given us a spirit of fear,
but of power and of love and of a sound mind.
2 Timothy 1:7

$\mathcal{D}$aily prayer for . . .
forgiveness

> *The Lord is slow to anger and rich*
> *in unfailing love, forgiving every kind*
> *of sin and rebellion.*
>
> Numbers 14:18 NLT

Dear Heavenly Father,

I want to be a dad who can say, "I'm sorry." I know it takes a lot of humility for a father to admit he is wrong, but I believe that kind of honesty will earn his children's true respect.

Help me remember that forgiveness starts with You, Lord. Whenever I make a poor choice that affects my family, quickly show me my sin so I can first fix my relationship with You. Then help me go to my family and ask their forgiveness.

As the head of my household, I know how important it is for me to model grace. Help me to always be as forgiving of others as You are.

Amen.

If we confess our sins, He is faithful and just to forgive us our sins.
1 John 1:9

MY PERSONAL PRAYER

When God pardons,
he consigns the offense to
everlasting forgetfulness.

Merv Rosell

Dear Father:

_____

_____

_____

_____

_____

_____

Amen

"Come now, and let us reason together,"
says the Lord, "Though your sins are like scarlet,
they shall be as white as snow."
Isaiah 1:18

Whoever believes in Him will receive remission of sins.
Acts 10:43

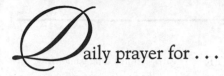aily prayer for . . .

protection

The Lord shall preserve you from all evil;
He shall preserve your soul.

Psalm 121:7

Dear Heavenly Father,

My children look so vulnerable when they're sleeping! I know that if they were ever in any danger, I would leap to defend them. But I can't go everywhere with them, and I can't defeat every threat. That's why it's so good to know that You can.

Please watch over them, Lord, and keep them from harm wherever they go, whatever they do. Guard them in every way—physically, mentally, emotionally, and spiritually. Protect their bodies from injury, their minds from lies, their hearts from wounds, and their souls from wandering.

My children feel safe around me, and I want them to always feel that way. So help me teach them that real security is found in You.

Amen.

May the name of the God of Jacob defend you.
Psalm 20:1

MY PERSONAL PRAYER

*If God maintains sun
and planets in bright and ordered
beauty he can keep us.*

F. B. Meyer

Dear Father:

_____

_____

_____

_____

_____

_____

Amen

*The Lord is faithful; he will make you strong
and guard you from the evil one.*
2 Thessalonians 3:3 NLT

*The name of the Lord is a strong tower;
the righteous run to it and are safe.*
Proverbs 18:10

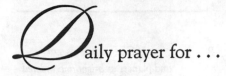

Daily prayer for . . .

courage

Be strong and of good courage; do not be afraid, nor be dismayed, for the Lord your God is with you wherever you go.

Joshua 1:9

Dear Heavenly Father,

Give me the kind of courage that will make my children proud of me and inspire courage in them. Make me a man who will face problems head-on. Make me a father who will stand for what is right, despite the consequences.

Make me bold enough to let my faith shine at all times—at home, at work, in public. Give me the courage to reach out to those rejected by others. Make me brave enough to share the gospel with someone who needs to hear it. Give me the confidence to build relationships with people who are different from me, people of other races, cultures, and social status.

Above all, give me the courage to love without reservation.

Amen.

In the day when I cried out, You answered me, and made me bold with strength in my soul.
Psalm 138:3

MY PERSONAL PRAYER

*Let us renew our trust in God
and go forward without fear and
with manly hearts.*

Abraham Lincoln

Dear Father:

_____

_____

_____

_____

_____

_____

Amen

Watch, stand fast in the faith, be brave, be strong.
1 Corinthians 16:13

The righteous are bold as a lion.
Proverbs 28:1

Daily prayer for . . .
strength

*Those who wait on the Lord shall renew
their strength; they shall mount up with
wings like eagles.*

Isaiah 40:31

Dear Heavenly Father,

Every man has areas in which he is strong, and others in
which he is weak. Some men are strong leaders; some are
not. Some are strong disciplinarians; others aren't. Men
who are good at teaching aren't always good at listening
or sympathizing. Guys who can fix anything don't always
know how to help solve homework problems.

Thank You for the natural strengths You have given
me. I know my unique set of gifts makes me a special
father. Help me make the most of these strengths and
build on them.

And, Lord, give me strength where I lack it. My children
need a father who is strong in all areas. I'm trusting in
Your power.

Amen.

Be strong in the grace that is in Christ Jesus.
2 Timothy 2:1

MY PERSONAL PRAYER

When God is our strength,
it is strength indeed.

Saint Augustine

Dear Father:

Amen

He will keep you strong right up to the end.
1 Corinthians 1:8 NLT

In quietness and confidence shall be your strength.
Isaiah 30:15

*D*aily prayer for . . .

rest

*He who has entered His rest has himself also
ceased from his works as God did from His.*

Hebrews 4:10

Dear Heavenly Father,

Every time my wife and I had another child, our world
started spinning faster. Now it's moving so quickly,
we've forgotten how to take a break. It's hard to find
time to rest, Lord! Our to-do lists won't even fit on our
daily planners.

Still, I know it's important for us to rest, for our sake
and our children's. It's not fair to them when we're so
overtaxed that we ignore them or snap at them.

So please help us to ink in the word *rest* on our
calendars—on Sundays, of course, but also regularly
throughout the week. Give us wisdom to know which
tasks can wait and which can be eliminated so we can
get the rest we need.

Amen.

*Ask for the old paths, where the good way is, and walk in it;
then you will find rest for your souls.*

Jeremiah 6:16

MY PERSONAL PRAYER

No sleep can be tranquil unless the mind is at rest.
Lucius Annaeus Seneca

Dear Father:

_____

_____

_____

_____

_____

_____

Amen

Jesus said, "Come to Me, all you who labor and are heavy laden, and I will give you rest."
Matthew 11:28

Rest in the Lord, and wait patiently for Him.
Psalm 37:7

$\mathcal{D}$aily prayer for . . .
hope

You are my hope, O Lord God;
You are my trust from my youth.

Psalm 71:5

Dear Heavenly Father,

Just like everyone else, I need hope to survive. But people put their hope in so many different things and are let down. I've been guilty myself of misplaced hope, and I've been disappointed too.

Give me the wisdom to know that You are the only true source of hope. Help me remember that building my life on Your promises is like building a home on solid rock. Don't let me be fooled anymore, Lord, by weak foundations that look stable.

I want to give my children hope, Father—a hope they can rely on. As I explain to them why I trust in You, help them understand. Open their eyes to the truth that You are the only sure foundation.

Amen.

You faithfully answer our prayers with awesome deeds,
O God our savior. You are the hope of everyone on earth.

Psalm 65:5 NLT

MY PERSONAL PRAYER

*The resurrection of Jesus Christ is
our hope today. It is our assurance
that we have a living Savior.*
Raymond MacKendree

Dear Father:

_____

_____

_____

_____

_____

_____

Amen

Hope in the Lord; for with the Lord there is mercy.
Psalm 130:7

*You are the God who saves me.
All day long I put my hope in you.*
Psalm 25:5 NLT

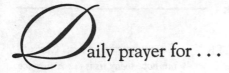

Daily prayer for . . .

patience

*He who is slow to anger is better than
the mighty, and he who rules his spirit than
he who takes a city.*

Proverbs 16:32

Dear Heavenly Father,

Before I had kids, I considered myself a patient man. Boy, was I wrong! I thought I'd learned all about patience; now I feel like I'm taking a graduate course in the subject.

It's amazing to me how a child I love so much can make me so angry so quickly. Because I love my child, I hate to see wrong behavior in them. But my impatience is sometimes due to selfishness, and for that I ask Your forgiveness.

Help me put my child's needs above mine, Lord. Give me the wisdom to plan my time so my need for speed doesn't clash with my child's slower pace. And when my child is disobedient, help me discipline them with patience and love.

Amen.

*May the Lord direct your hearts into the love of God
and into the patience of Christ.*

2 Thessalonians 3:5

MY PERSONAL PRAYER

Patience is the companion
of wisdom.

Saint Augustine

Dear Father:

_____

_____

_____

_____

_____

_____

Amen

The patient in spirit is better than the proud in spirit.
Ecclesiastes 7:8

Be patient in trouble, and always be prayerful.
Romans 12:12 NLT

$\mathcal{D}$aily prayer for . . .

contentment

> *The fear of the Lord leads to life, and he*
> *who has it will abide in satisfaction.*
>
> Proverbs 19:23

Dear Heavenly Father,

I need help figuring out how to be content and stay motivated at the same time. I find that every time I start feeling content, my wife complains that nothing is getting done around the house! There must be a good balance there somewhere; please reveal it to me.

Discontentment touches many areas of my life. At different times I feel dissatisfied with my job, my home, my car, my friends and family, even my golf game. The apostle Paul claimed to have discovered the secret of being content in any situation, and that's astounding to me. Please show me the secret of contentment as well. It's something I need, and it's something I want to pass along to my children.

Amen.

> *Be content with such things as you have. For He Himself has said,*
> *"I will never leave you nor forsake you."*
>
> Hebrews 13:5

MY PERSONAL PRAYER

Contentment is realizing that God has already given me everything I need for my present happiness.

Bill Gothard

Dear Father:

_____

_____

_____

_____

_____

_____

Amen

Oh, satisfy us early with Your mercy,
that we may rejoice and be glad all our days!
Psalm 90:14

Godliness with contentment is great gain.
1 Timothy 6:6

*D*aily prayer for . . .
faith

Faith is the substance of things hoped for,
the evidence of things not seen.

Hebrews 11:1

Dear Heavenly Father,

Faith is a bit of a mystery to me. I'm not sure to what extent it's a gift from You, and to what extent it's our response to You. I'm sure it's a combination of both. I do know I have a measure of faith, however small, and You've rewarded it far out of proportion. Thank You, Lord.

I know You want me to have more faith, to trust You more with my family, my career, and my life. I want more faith too. So to the extent that faith is a gift from You, please increase my faith. And to the extent that it's our response to You, give me courage to take the next step of faith You're calling me to take.

Amen.

Looking unto Jesus, the author and finisher of our faith.

Hebrews 12:2

MY PERSONAL PRAYER

Faith is a reasoning trust,
a trust which reckons
thoughtfully and confidently upon
the trustworthiness of God.
John R. W. Stott

Dear Father:

_____

_____

_____

_____

_____

_____

Amen

By faith you stand.
2 Corinthians 1:24

The just shall live by faith.
Romans 1:17

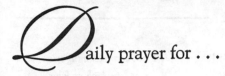

aily prayer for . . .

perseverance

> *You have need of endurance, so that after*
> *you have done the will of God, you may*
> *receive the promise.*
>
> Hebrews 10:36

Dear Heavenly Father,

One of the most important lessons a father can teach his children is to keep striving until the goal is achieved. I want to teach my children this concept, but I struggle with it myself.

It seems the only way to learn perseverance is to practice it. So help me persevere in every area of my life, especially in my spiritual growth. Give me the discipline I need to stick with my daily times of Bible study and prayer. Then my children will not only hear me talk about perseverance but see it in my life.

Help them as they attempt to finish their first big projects. Bless them with a feeling of accomplishment that will motivate them to always persevere.

Amen.

> *Tribulation produces perseverance; and perseverance,*
> *character; and character, hope.*
>
> Romans 5:3–4

MY PERSONAL PRAYER

*Perseverance is the rope that ties
the soul to the doorpost of heaven.*
Frances J. Roberts

Dear Father:

_____

_____

_____

_____

_____

Amen

Let us run with endurance the race that is set before us.
Hebrews 12:1

*If we hope for what we do not see,
we eagerly wait for it with perseverance.*
Romans 8:25

$\mathcal{D}$aily prayer for . . .

purpose

*I cry out to God Most High, to God who
will fulfill his purpose for me.*

Psalm 57:2 NLT

Dear Heavenly Father,

At times I'm overwhelmed by life's monotony.
Sometimes it seems I just keep doing the same things
over and over, and it's hard to find any meaning to it all.

Remind me that what I'm doing helps fulfill Your grand
purpose. Every day as I provide for, take care of, and
interact with my children, You are using me to shape
their character. Although I'm often unable to see the
progress, it's always obvious from Your perspective.

When the daily grind gets me down, help me remember
the workers who carved Mount Rushmore. For years they
labored up close, chipping away at the rock, unable to see
the big picture. Yet slowly but surely they transformed
the mountain into a monument.

Amen.

*All things work together for good to those who love God,
to those who are the called according to His purpose.*

Romans 8:28

MY PERSONAL PRAYER

*Nothing in this world is
without meaning.*

A. W. Tozer

Dear Father:

_____

_____

_____

_____

_____

_____

Amen

*We are His workmanship, created in Christ Jesus
for good works, which God prepared beforehand
that we should walk in them.*
Ephesians 2:10

He who does the will of God abides forever.
1 John 2:17

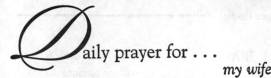

Daily prayer for . . .
my wife

Who can find a virtuous wife? For her
worth is far above rubies.

Proverbs 31:10

Dear Heavenly Father,

My spouse is such a wonderful gift from You. I confess that too often I've taken her for granted. Help me value her more. Open my eyes to see what a blessing she is, both as a wife to me and as a mother to our children.

Thank You for the strengths You have given her, and for the way our personalities complement each other. Help us work as a team, fulfilling the individual roles You have assigned us.

Make me a blessing to her as a husband. Help me meet her needs as much as I can; at the same time, Lord, remind her to always look to You to meet the needs only You can fulfill.

Amen.

Rejoice with the wife of your youth . . .
Always be enraptured with her love.
Proverbs 5:18–19

MY PERSONAL PRAYER

In romanticism, [a woman] is the fairy princess or maiden in distress waiting to be rescued; in biblical faith, she is the partner in ministry.

Donald G. Bloesch

Dear Father:

_____

_____

_____

_____

_____

_____

Amen

A woman who fears the Lord, she shall be praised.
Proverbs 31:30

A worthy wife is her husband's joy and crown.
Proverbs 12:4 NLT

*D*aily prayer for . . .
my children

Children are a heritage from the Lord,
the fruit of the womb is a reward.

Psalm 127:3

Dear Heavenly Father,

Sometimes I think my house has been invaded by aliens;
sometimes I feel as if we've been visited by angels.
Children have brought all kinds of craziness into my life,
but they've sure brought a lot of blessings as well.

Someone has said that children beget adults, and I believe
that's true. Thank You, Lord, for the way You have used
my kids to mature me. At the same time, thank You for
how You have used them to keep me young.

Bless my little ones today and every day of their lives.
Protect them, provide for them, and draw them closer
to You. I commit them to Your keeping, and trust that
You will never let them go.

Amen.

The righteous man walks in his integrity;
his children are blessed after him.

Proverbs 20:7

MY PERSONAL PRAYER

Children are God's apostles,
day by day sent forth to preach
of love, and hope, and peace.
James Russell Lowell

Dear Father:

_____

_____

_____

_____

_____

_____

Amen

The father of godly children has cause for joy.
Proverbs 23:24 NLT

The love of the Lord remains forever with those who fear
him. His salvation extends to the children's children.
Psalm 103:17

$\mathcal{D}$aily prayer for . . .

my siblings

> *Esau ran up and embraced [his brother Jacob], held him tight and kissed him.*
>
> Genesis 33:4 MSG

Dear Heavenly Father,

My siblings have been such an important part of my life. It's always good to talk to them, because we share so much history and know each other so well.

Thank You for the way I can laugh with them about old times, and for how their insight helps me understand myself better. Thank You that You've given me someone to call when I'm feeling a little lonely or need some advice. Help me to be there for them when they need me.

Show me how to teach my own children how to be there for each other, how to support one another in the same way.

Amen.

> *How wonderful it is, how pleasant,*
> *when brothers live together in harmony!*
> Psalm 133:1 NLT

MY PERSONAL PRAYER

*The family circle is the supreme
conductor of Christianity.*

Henry Drummond

Dear Father:

_____

_____

_____

_____

_____

_____

Amen

A brother is born for adversity.
Proverbs 17:17

Be kindly affectionate to one another with brotherly love.
Romans 12:10

$\mathcal{D}$aily prayer for . . .

my parents

Let your father and your mother be glad,
and let her who bore you rejoice.

Proverbs 23:25

Dear Heavenly Father,

Thank You for the parents You gave me. Help me communicate my gratitude to them. And help me honor them, in my interactions with them and in how I live my life.

As good as my folks were and are to me, nobody's perfect. So help me forgive them where necessary—and vice versa—so we'll always be on good terms.

Lord, as my mom and dad grow older, it's becoming my turn to look after them. Help me meet their needs even as I raise my own children. Remind me to call and visit often.

Bless my parents' relationship with my kids; help them to be good grandparents. Keep them in good health physically and spiritually for the rest of their lives.

Amen.

Honor your father and your mother,
as the Lord your God has commanded you.

Deuteronomy 5:16

MY PERSONAL PRAYER

*We never know the love of
the parent until we become
parents ourselves.*

Henry Ward Beecher

Dear Father:

_____

_____

_____

_____

_____

_____

Amen

Whoever loves wisdom makes his father rejoice.
Proverbs 29:3

Parents are the pride of their children.
Proverbs 17:6 NLT

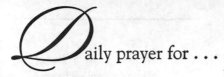

Daily prayer for . . .
my friends

Two are better than one...For if they fall,
one will lift up his companion.

Ecclesiastes 4:9–10

Dear Heavenly Father,

I've known some of my friends since childhood, others only a short time. Some live nearby, some far away. They're different in so many respects. Help me to be a true friend to each one.

Bless my friends in every way, Lord. Protect them. Wherever they are spiritually, draw them nearer to You. Reveal yourself to them more each day.

Remind me to cultivate my friendships. I'm not as good as my wife at keeping in touch with people and letting them know I care. Friends drift apart, and I wouldn't want to lose someone I love.

Help me share my faith with my nonbelieving friends. Give me the courage to risk my relationships in the hope that they'll extend into eternity.

Amen.

I am a companion of all who fear You, and of those who keep Your precepts.
Psalm 119:63

MY PERSONAL PRAYER

*Blessed are they who have the gift
of making friends, for it is one of
God's best gifts.*

Thomas Hughes

Dear Father:

_____

_____

_____

_____

_____

_____

Amen

There is a friend who sticks closer than a brother.
Proverbs 18:24

A friend loves at all times.
Proverbs 17:17

$\mathcal{D}$aily prayer for . . .
my enemies

Jesus said, "Love your enemies,
bless those who curse you."

Matthew 5:44

Dear Heavenly Father,

There are people who oppose me in different ways—at work, in the neighborhood, even at church. To some extent I consider them enemies. Help me to love them and work toward making them friends.

Some people in my country fight against causes I care about deeply. The moral issues involved seem crystal clear to me, and it's hard to relate to these people. Give me courage and wisdom to stand for what's right, Lord, but also help me to value and respect every person. Help me teach my children to do likewise.

Help me forgive those who've hurt me in the past, so I can stop considering them my enemies. I want to carry love, not bitterness, in my heart.

Amen.

If your enemy is hungry, give him bread to eat;
and if he is thirsty, give him water to drink.
Proverbs 25:21

MY PERSONAL PRAYER

If we could read the secret history of our enemies, we should find in each man's life sorrow and suffering enough to disarm all hostility.

Henry Wadsworth Longfellow

Dear Father:

_____

_____

_____

_____

_____

_____

Amen

Jesus said, "For if you forgive men their trespasses, your heavenly Father will also forgive you."
Matthew 6:14

Do not be overcome by evil, but overcome evil with good.
Romans 12:21

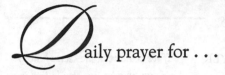

Daily prayer for . . .

my community

*By the blessing of the upright the
city is exalted.*

Proverbs 11:11

Dear Heavenly Father,

Help me look beyond my property lines and see the people in my neighborhood and community. Help me care about them the way You do.

Remind me to pray for the people I see around me every day. There are folks in my neighborhood I haven't met, yet I wave at them regularly as I drive past their houses. Give me and my family the chance to get to know some of them better, so we can show them Your love.

You told Abraham that You would spare an entire city for the sake of a few godly people. Make us such people, Lord. Help me lead my wife and kids in upholding our community through faithful living and prayer.

Amen.

Unless the Lord guards the city, the watchman stays awake in vain.
Psalm 127:1

MY PERSONAL PRAYER

The Christian life was not meant to
live in a solitude…It is a social life.
Phillips Brooks

Dear Father:

_____

_____

_____

_____

_____

_____

Amen

Happy are the people whose God is the Lord!
Psalm 144:15

When it goes well with the righteous, the city rejoices.
Proverbs 11:10

$\mathcal{D}$aily prayer for . . .
my church

Christ is head of the church;
and He is the Savior of the body.
Ephesians 5:23

Dear Heavenly Father,

I've heard about the Brooklyn Tabernacle, and other churches, where prayer has made such a difference. Help me remember how important prayer is to the life of a church.

As I pray for my church, give me faith to believe You will answer. Help me to always live righteously, so my prayers will be strong and effective, as the Bible promises.

Motivate others in my congregation to begin praying too, Lord. I want my church to be alive with Your Spirit—a place where my children and others will sense Your presence, feel Your power, and be drawn to Your love. I know this will only happen if the people of my church faithfully pray for You to bless us.

Amen.

Now you are the body of Christ, and members individually.
1 Corinthians 12:27

MY PERSONAL PRAYER

What matters in the church is not religion but the form of Christ, and its taking form amidst a band of men.

Dietrich Bonhoeffer

Dear Father:

_____

_____

_____

_____

_____

_____

Amen

Christ also loved the church and gave Himself for her, that He might sanctify and cleanse her.
Ephesians 5:25-26

To [God] be glory in the church by Christ Jesus to all generations.
Ephesians 3:21

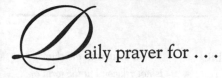

Daily prayer for . . .

our schools

Train up a child in the way he should go, and
when he is old he will not depart from it.

Proverbs 22:6

Dear Heavenly Father,

They say You have been kicked out of the public schools. But I know You would never give up on our children. You told the apostle Paul, "Do not be afraid . . . I have many people in this city"; I trust that You have many godly teachers, administrators, and staff in our public schools. Use them in powerful ways to impact the lives of our young ones.

Protect all our schools, public and private. Make them into safe places for physical, emotional, and intellectual growth. Help children learn the social skills they need; teach them to relate to their teachers and each other with respect. Use the schools to mold our children into citizens who will make a difference in our world.

Amen.

The law of the wise is a fountain of life.
Proverbs 13:14

MY PERSONAL PRAYER

A teacher affects eternity; he can never tell where his influence stops.
Henry Adams

Dear Father:

_____

_____

_____

_____

_____

_____

Amen

Happy is the man who finds wisdom,
and the man who gains understanding.
Proverbs 3:13

Wisdom is better than rubies, and all the things
one may desire cannot be compared with her.
Proverbs 8:11

$\mathcal{D}$aily prayer for . . .

our country

Blessed is the nation whose God is the Lord.
Psalm 33:12

Dear Heavenly Father,

I pray that the people of this country will recognize You as the one true God and begin to trust and obey You. If we do, Lord, so many of our problems will be solved. It's Your hand on this nation that makes it great.

Help me join the other Christians who pray regularly for this country. We need You, Father! Guide us. Provide for our needs. Help us prosper. Protect us from those who want to harm us. And set this country once again on its historical foundation, which is faith in You.

Jesus said the truth will set us free. Show us the true path to liberty. I want my children to inherit a country that is free indeed.

Amen.

If My people . . . will humble themselves, and pray . . . then I will hear from heaven, and will forgive their sin and heal their land.
2 Chronicles 7:14

MY PERSONAL PRAYER

The strength of a country is the
strength of its religious convictions.
Calvin Coolidge

Dear Father:

_____

_____

_____

_____

_____

_____

Amen

Righteousness exalts a nation.
Proverbs 14:34

He shall speak peace to the nations;
His dominion shall be . . . to the ends of the earth.
Zechariah 9:10

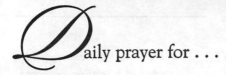 aily prayer for . . .

our world

The Father has sent the Son
as Savior of the world.

1 John 4:14

Dear Heavenly Father,

Jesus taught us to pray that Your will would be done on earth, the way it is in heaven. That's the kind of world I want my children to grow up in!

Your will for this earth is perfect, and the Bible makes much of it very clear. So today I pray that people around the world will begin to seek justice, help the oppressed, comfort the brokenhearted, care for widows and orphans, feed the hungry, provide shelter for the homeless, clothe the naked, tend to the sick, visit prisoners, and share the gospel.

Thank You that all over the planet, members of Your church are already doing these things in obedience and love. Bless them and their work, Lord.

Amen.

The earth is the Lord's, and all its fullness,
the world and those who dwell therein.

Psalm 24:1

MY PERSONAL PRAYER

Far from turning us away from the world, Christ directs us to it. He awakens within us an altogether new concern for it.

Paul Tournier

Dear Father:

_____

_____

_____

_____

_____

_____

Amen

Let all the earth fear the Lord;
let all the inhabitants of the world stand in awe of Him.
Psalm 33:8

Be exalted, O God, above the heavens,
and Your glory above all the earth.
Psalm 108:5

_D_aily prayer for . . .

my work

_Let the beauty of the Lord our God
be upon us, and establish the work of
our hands for us._

Psalm 90:17

Dear Heavenly Father,

So much of my life revolves around my job. I know
work is a gift from You, but help me balance my work
and my home life. My wife and children need me too.

I want my work to have eternal significance. So I'm
dedicating it to You, Lord, and I'm committing a portion
of my income to You. Use my labor and money however
You wish. I pray that it will help build up Your church
and touch people's lives.

Perhaps some person will decide today to follow Jesus
because of a ministry supported by the work I do. Help
me keep that thought in mind as I do my job. Enable
me to do my best for Your glory.

Amen.

Whatever you do, do it heartily, as to the Lord.
Colossians 3:23

MY PERSONAL PRAYER

*The work an unknown good man
has done is like a vein of water
flowing hidden underground,
making the ground green.*

Thomas Carlyle

Dear Father:

_____

_____

_____

_____

_____

_____

Amen

*When you eat the labor of your hands,
you shall be happy, and it shall be well with you.*
Psalm 128:2

O God, strengthen my hands.
Nehemiah 6:9

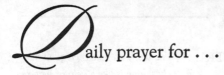

Daily prayer for . . .
my ministry

*Jesus said, "Go therefore and make
disciples of all the nations."*

Matthew 28:19

Dear Heavenly Father,

Thank You for this ministry. Thank You for the spiritual
gifts that make me suitable for it. Thank You also for
putting a passion in my heart for the people this ministry
touches. Keep that passion burning brightly, Lord.

I know that whatever good this ministry accomplishes is
because of You, and I give You all the glory for it. Help
me never to seek recognition or praise for my work, but
simply to be grateful for the blessing I get from being
part of what You're doing in the world.

Bless what I'm doing for Your kingdom. I commit my
life to serving You by ministering to others, and pray my
example will be an inspiration to my children.

Amen.

*Since we have this ministry, as we have received mercy,
we do not lose heart.*

2 Corinthians 4:1

MY PERSONAL PRAYER

Attempt great things for God;
expect great things from God.
William Carey

Dear Father:

_____

_____

_____

_____

_____

_____

_____

Amen

Jesus said, "You shall receive power when the Holy Spirit has
come upon you; and you shall be witnesses to Me."
Acts 1:8

Be steadfast, immovable, always abounding in the work of
the Lord, knowing that your labor is not in vain in the Lord.
1 Corinthians 15:58

Large asking and large expectations
on our part honor God.

A. L. Stone

Daily Prayers for Help . . .

Daily prayer for help . . .
when I'm struggling with sin

Jesus said, "Watch and pray, lest you enter into temptation."

Matthew 26:41

Dear Heavenly Father,

When I'm tempted to sin, help me remember that winning this battle will result in blessings not only to me but also to my wife and children and to the generations to follow. That should be enough to motivate any man to beat temptation! But even better, my victory over sin will please and honor You.

I need this kind of positive motivation as I face temptation, because it can be so enticing. I get tricked into thinking I'm being deprived of something good. Help me to recognize this lie, and put my trust in You, because Your promises are far greater than anything the devil has to offer.

My children are watching me, Lord. Keep me strong and wise.

Amen.

God is faithful. He will keep the temptation from becoming so strong that you can't stand up against it.
1 Corinthians 10:13 NLT

MY PERSONAL PRAYER

*Unless there is within us that which
is above us, we shall soon yield to
that which is about us.*

P. T. Forsyth

Dear Father:

_____

_____

_____

_____

_____

_____

Amen

Do not lead us into temptation.
Luke 11:4

*When you are tempted, [God] will show you a way out so
that you will not give in to it.*
1 Corinthians 10:13 NLT

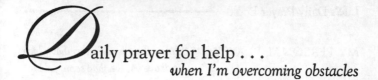

$\mathcal{D}$aily prayer for help . . .
when I'm overcoming obstacles

*Thanks be to God, who gives us the victory
through our Lord Jesus Christ.*

1 Corinthians 15:57

Dear Heavenly Father,

Ever since Adam, we guys have been dealing with weeds and thorns.

I struggle with obstacles at work and at home, in my spiritual life and in trying to be a good husband and father. Many of these obstacles are simply annoying, but some seem overwhelming.

Give me patience and self-control when I get frustrated over little things that get in my way. Help me not to sin when I'm annoyed. I want to teach my children how to handle life's problems well.

When I'm intimidated by a problem that looks insurmountable, give me wisdom, courage, and strength to overcome it. I trust You to help me conquer all the obstacles in my life, or to remove them from my path.

Amen.

Jesus said, "Take heart, because I have overcome the world."
John 16:33 NLT

MY PERSONAL PRAYER

*Nothing great was ever done
without much enduring.*

Catherine of Siena

Dear Father:

_____

_____

_____

_____

_____

_____

Amen

We count them blessed who endure.
James 5:11

By my God I can leap over a wall.
Psalm 18:29

Daily prayer for help . . .
when I'm dealing with grief

*Weeping may endure for a night, but joy
comes in the morning.*

Psalm 30:5

Dear Heavenly Father,

Help me deal with the pain I feel inside. I can tough it out when I get hurt physically, but I'm not sure how to handle this grief.

Sometimes it's so intense I want to cry, but often that doesn't seem appropriate. Lord, help me in those times not to allow my pain to cause me to lash out at others, especially my wife and children. Help me draw close to my loved ones instead of pulling away from them. Help me talk to them about my feelings instead of bottling them up inside.

Thank You for walking beside me and my family during this difficult time. I sense Your comforting presence, and it's giving us all reassurance and hope.

Amen.

Blessed are those who mourn, for they shall be comforted.
Matthew 5:4

MY PERSONAL PRAYER

There is only one being who can satisfy the last aching abyss of the human heart, and that is the Lord Jesus Christ.

Oswald Chambers

Dear Father:

_____

_____

_____

_____

_____

_____

Amen

The Lord is near to those who have a broken heart.
Psalm 34:18

God will wipe away every tear from their eyes.
Revelation 21:4

Daily prayer for help . . .
when I need direction

The Lord is my shepherd; I shall not want....
He leads me in the paths of righteousness.
Psalm 23:1, 3

Dear Heavenly Father,

I've come to trust You and believe that You want only the best for me. I'm committed to following Your will for my life. Please guide me as I lead my family. I need Your direction as I make choices that will impact all of our lives.

Thank You for giving me my wife to help me make important decisions. Remind me to listen to and value her input. Help us remember to pray over all these matters. Verify Your will for us by bringing us to a point where we're in agreement about the way to go. I know You want us to be a team. Help us both to hear Your voice and have the faith to obey it.

Amen.

Your ears shall hear a word behind you, saying,
"This is the way, walk in it."
Isaiah 30:21

MY PERSONAL PRAYER

God shall be my hope, my stay,
my guide, and lantern to my feet.
William Shakespeare

Dear Father:

_____

_____

_____

_____

_____

_____

Amen

Jesus said, "My sheep hear My voice,
and I know them, and they follow Me."
John 10:27

He is our God forever and ever, and he will be our guide.
Psalm 48:14 NLT

*D*aily prayer for help . . .
when I have financial needs

> *God shall supply all your need according to His riches in glory by Christ Jesus.*
>
> Philippians 4:19

Dear Heavenly Father,

I explained to my seven-year-old, who never turns off the lights, that *everything* costs money. He reminded me about air, and I said I'm confident somebody will figure out how to charge for that too.

Lord, my wife and I are trying hard to manage our money in a way that will honor You. Help us live within the means You provide us. Give us the faith to return to You a portion of our income, trusting You to meet all our needs.

Remind us to always serve You, not money. Make us good stewards of our resources. Help us teach our children the godly way to manage their piggy banks now, so they can wisely handle checking accounts later.

Amen.

> *Seek first the kingdom of God and His righteousness, and all these things shall be added to you.*
>
> Matthew 6:33

MY PERSONAL PRAYER

*Human problems are never
greater than divine solutions.*

Erwin W. Lutzer

Dear Father:

_____

_____

_____

_____

_____

_____

Amen

Cast your burden on the Lord, and He shall sustain you.
Psalm 55:22

*God says, "Call upon Me in the day of trouble;
I will deliver you."*
Psalm 50:15

*D*aily prayer for help . . .
when I'm depressed

> *Evening and morning and at noon I will pray,*
> *and cry aloud, and He shall hear my voice.*
>
> Psalm 55:17

Dear Heavenly Father,

So often my emotional state of mind is linked to my faith. Someone has said that if you believe in God, everything is miraculous; if you don't, nothing is. When my faith is strong, I see Your glory everywhere and I'm very optimistic. Yet when I begin to doubt, everything looks bleak and I sink into despair.

It reminds me of Peter walking to Jesus on the water. As long as he kept his eyes on Christ, he experienced the miraculous. But when he looked away, he began to descend into the sea. Lord Jesus, grab my hand and pull me up, because I'm sinking again. Forgive me for doubting, as Peter did. Help me stay focused on You and believe.

Amen.

> *[God] reached down from heaven and rescued me;*
> *he drew me out of deep waters.*
> 2 Samuel 22:17 NLT

MY PERSONAL PRAYER

*I have plumbed the depths
of despair and found them
not bottomless.*

Thomas Hardy

Dear Father:

_____

_____

_____

_____

_____

_____

Amen

I love the Lord, because He has heard my voice.
Psalm 116:1

*God led me to a place of safety;
he rescued me because he delights in me.*
Psalm 18:19 NLT

$\mathcal{D}$aily prayer for help . . .
when I'm struggling with doubt

"You don't have much faith," Jesus said.
"Why did you doubt me?"
Matthew 14:31 NLT

Dear Heavenly Father,

Since doubt always leads to despair, help me understand why I begin to question my faith. This is so important, Lord, because when I'm down, it affects not only me but also my family.

I know there are two ways of looking at the world—through unbelief and through faith—and I must choose which lens to use. Help me figure out why I sometimes pick up the unbelieving lens. Reveal to me the things that trigger doubt in my heart, and give me the wisdom to quickly reject them.

Help me always view my world through the lens of faith. It's not rose-colored; it allows me to see everything as it really is. So it allows me to see You.

Amen.

"Lord, I believe; help my unbelief!"
Mark 9:24

MY PERSONAL PRAYER

Every step toward Christ kills a doubt. Every thought, word, and deed for him carries you away from discouragement.

Theodore Ledyard Cuyler

Dear Father:

_____

_____

_____

_____

_____

_____

Amen

The apostles said to the Lord, "Increase our faith."
Luke 17:5

Jesus said, "I have prayed for you, that your faith should not fail."
Luke 22:32

Daily prayer for help . . .
when I'm facing persecution

Blessed are those who are persecuted for righteousness'
sake, for theirs is the kingdom of heaven.

Matthew 5:10

Dear Heavenly Father,

It's easy to tell when people think less of me because of my faith. Sometimes they're openly scornful. Although it hurts to lose people's respect, help me never to disown You in any way to win their approval. You are worth any humiliation I might endure.

The apostle Paul wrote that the "light afflictions" Christians face are nothing compared with our reward in heaven. I know my troubles are pretty minor, especially when I consider how other Christians suffer. Help me deal with the small persecutions I face, but even more so, strengthen and encourage persecuted Christians around the world.

Lord, my children are starting to experience the sting of persecution as well. Help them glorify You through it.

Amen.

Count it all joy when you fall into various trials,
knowing that the testing of your faith produces patience.

James 1:2–3

MY PERSONAL PRAYER

The prophet and the martyr do not
see the hooting throng. Their eyes
are fixed on the eternities.

Benjamin N. Cardozo

Dear Father:

_____

_____

_____

_____

_____

_____

_____

Amen

These trials are only to test your faith,
to show that it is strong and pure.
1 Peter 1:7 NLT

Jesus said, "The world would love you if you belonged to it,
but you don't. I chose you to come out of the world."
John 15:19 NLT

Daily prayer for help . . .
when I've been rejected

He was despised and rejected—a man of
sorrows, acquainted with bitterest grief.
Isaiah 53:3 NLT

Dear Heavenly Father,

I try not to take it personally when my idea at work gets rejected in favor of an associate's, or I get passed over for a promotion and my coworker gets it. Sometimes it's hard, though. Old feelings of rejection flood my mind, and I wind up feeling hurt and angry.

Perhaps my childhood memories come back so easily because I'm watching my kids deal with rejection. Somebody always seems to get left out when children play. Kids get hurt and angry too; they just don't hide it!

Lord Jesus, you know what it's like to be rejected. You handled rejection perfectly, without sinning. Help me and my children to be like You, especially when we're rejected because of our faith.

Amen.

Jesus said, "He who rejects you rejects Me,
and he who rejects Me rejects Him who sent Me."
Luke 10:16

MY PERSONAL PRAYER

It is preferable to have the whole world against thee, than Jesus offended with thee.

Thomas à Kempis

Dear Father:

_____

_____

_____

_____

_____

_____

Amen

Christ has accepted you.
Romans 15:7 NLT

*We know that God loves you . . .
and that he chose you to be his own people.*
1 Thessalonians 1:4 NLT

Daily prayer for help . . .
when I'm physically ill

> O Lord my God, I cried out to You,
> and You healed me.
>
> Psalm 30:2

Dear Heavenly Father,

This is such a busy time of life for my wife and me, and when one of us or the children gets sick, it becomes a hardship for the whole family.

Please heal me of this illness as quickly as possible, so I can resume doing my job, helping around the house, and serving in my ministry. In the meantime, relieve my symptoms enough so I can care for myself and not be a burden on my wife. Give her the energy she needs to handle the kids and the housework by herself while I recover.

Protect my wife and children from getting sick too. Help us all practice healthy habits so we can enjoy life-long good health.

Amen.

Jesus was moved with compassion for them, and healed their sick.
Matthew 14:14

MY PERSONAL PRAYER

There are no colds in Paradise. So, healing of any kind is . . . a direct expression and furtherance of God's will. It means bringing life back to what it ought to be.

Evelyn Underhill

Dear Father:

_____

_____

_____

_____

_____

_____

Amen

God says, "To you who fear My name the Sun of Righteousness shall arise with healing in His wings."
Malachi 4:2

I pray that you may prosper in all things and be in health, just as your soul prospers.
3 John 1:2

Daily prayer for help . . .

when I'm fearful

Give all your worries and cares to God,
for he cares about what happens to you.
1 Peter 5:7 NLT

Dear Heavenly Father,

The daily news gives me plenty of reasons to fear for my family's safety and well-being. Remind me that You are in control, Lord. I trust that no matter what You allow to happen in this world, You will work it all out for good for those who believe.

Sometimes this sounds a bit trite to me. But the only alternative to trusting You is to either try to be courageous on my own or live a life motivated by fear. I'm not strong enough to face the world alone; too much of it is out of my control. And I want to be motivated by love. So I'm putting my faith in You. I'm glad You're worthy of it.

Amen.

Jesus said, "Let not your heart be troubled, neither let it be afraid."
John 14:27

MY PERSONAL PRAYER

A perfect faith would lift us
absolutely above fear.

George Macdonald

Dear Father:

_____

_____

_____

_____

_____

_____

Amen

The Lord is on my side; I will not fear.
Psalm 118:6

If God is for us, who can be against us?
Romans 8:31

*D*aily prayer for help . . .
when my marriage is in trouble

*Let us not love in word or in tongue,
but in deed and in truth.*

1 John 3:18

Dear Heavenly Father,

I'm amazed that my marriage can be so fragile and yet so strong. Sometimes one wrong word is enough to upset the apple cart. Yet my marriage has endured so much over the years. I give You the credit for that, Lord. I'm thankful that my wife and I chose to build our marriage on Your foundation.

Father, there are apples all over the floor right now. Please help us sort through this mess. If this issue's too big for us to handle alone, give us the wisdom to get counseling. Help us reassure the kids that we'll be okay.

My wife and I love each other very much. But we need You to help us show one another our love.

Amen.

*[Christ] Himself is our peace, who has made both one,
and has broken down the middle wall of separation.*
Ephesians 2:14

MY PERSONAL PRAYER

Successful marriage is always
a triangle: a man, a woman,
and God.

Cecil Myers

Dear Father:

_____

_____

_____

_____

_____

_____

Amen

Be good husbands to your wives.
Honor them, delight in them.
1 Peter 3:7 MSG

Love never gives up, never loses faith, is always hopeful, and
endures through every circumstance. Love will last forever.
1 Corinthians 13:7–8 NLT

$\mathcal{D}$aily prayer for help . . .
when I'm struggling at work

> *Commit your work to the Lord, and then*
> *your plans will succeed.*
>
> Proverbs 16:3 NLT

Dear Heavenly Father,

I need Your help to be more efficient in my job. It's a challenge to maintain both the speed and the quality expected of me, but I need to find a way. Give me wisdom, Lord, and energy to work hard. In today's competitive environment, the company could lose valuable clients if I miss deadlines or deliver inferior work. My wife and kids depend on me, so I'm depending on You.

Help me also to get along better with my supervisor and fellow workers. Sometimes the stresses of the workplace put a real strain on relationships. That just makes the productivity problem worse. Bless the people where I work, and help me do my part to foster goodwill in my department.

Amen.

> *The hand of the diligent will rule.*
> Proverbs 12:24

MY PERSONAL PRAYER

Work, work, from early until late.
In fact, I have so much to do
that I shall spend the first three
hours in prayer.

Martin Luther

Dear Father:

_____

_____

_____

_____

_____

_____

Amen

In all labor there is profit.
Proverbs 14:23

You will keep him in perfect peace,
whose mind is stayed on You.
Isaiah 26:3

*D*aily prayer for help . . .
when I need to confront someone

*They should gently teach those who oppose
the truth. Perhaps God will change those
people's hearts.*

2 Timothy 2:25 NLT

Dear Heavenly Father,

I need to talk to a friend about some sin in his life, and
I'm worried about how he'll respond. I don't want to
confront him, but nobody else has, and I'm afraid his
actions are going to harm him and his family.

Before I speak to him, please confirm that I should. Then
help me find the right words to express my concern. I
don't want to come across as holier-than-thou. Prepare
our hearts for this conversation. Help my friend know
that I sincerely care about him.

I don't know what his relationship with You is like right
now. Help me get to know him better so I can encourage
him in his faith.

Amen.

Rebuke one who has understanding, and he will discern knowledge.
Proverbs 19:25

MY PERSONAL PRAYER

Criticism, like rain, should be
gentle enough to nourish a man's
growth without destroying his roots.
Frank A. Clark

Dear Father:

_____

_____

_____

_____

_____

_____

Amen

As iron sharpens iron,
so a man sharpens the countenance of his friend.
Proverbs 27:17

If a man is overtaken in any trespass, you who are
spiritual restore such a one in a spirit of gentleness.
Galatians 6:1

*D*aily prayer for help . . .
when I can't sleep

> *I will both lie down in peace, and sleep; for*
> *You alone, O Lord, make me dwell in safety.*
> Psalm 4:8

Dear Heavenly Father,

I'm really wound up tonight. I'm exhausted but my
mind is racing. There's so much going on in my life
right now, both good and bad, that I can't seem to settle
down and fall asleep.

The house is quiet; my wife and kids are sleeping. I
need to get some rest, because I have a full day tomorrow.
So calm my mind, Lord. I commit myself and my loved
ones into Your hands. I give You all my worries. Replace
them with soothing thoughts about You.

Meditating on Your Word always eases my mind and
helps me rest. Help me remember the Scripture passages
I've memorized that will put peace in my heart, both
now and in the days ahead.

Amen.

> *[The Lord] gives His beloved sleep.*
> Psalm 127:2

MY PERSONAL PRAYER

Don't count sheep if you can't sleep. Talk to the shepherd.

Paul Frost

Dear Father:

_____

_____

_____

_____

_____

_____

Amen

*Those who live in the shelter of the Most High
will find rest in the shadow of the Almighty.*
Psalm 91:1 NLT

I lay down and slept; I awoke, for the Lord sustained me.
Psalm 3:5

*D*aily prayer for help . . .

when I'm angry

*Don't sin by letting anger gain
control over you.*

Psalm 4:4 NLT

Dear Heavenly Father,

Thank you for the Psalms. Because they're so honest, I feel free to speak frankly to You when I'm angry with my wife or one of my children.

It's good to talk to You because You listen, You care, and You aren't bothered by my raw emotions. Help me calm down now and begin to see things from Your perspective. Give me understanding so I can figure out what to do about the situation.

Thank You for letting me pour out my feelings to You when I'm upset. It's the best way I've found to deal with anger. Later I'll be able to talk rationally with the person I'm angry at, and we can work constructively together to resolve the conflict.

Amen.

Cease from anger, and forsake wrath; do not fret—it only causes harm.
Psalm 37:8

MY PERSONAL PRAYER

People who fly into a rage always make a bad landing.

Will Rogers

Dear Father:

_____

_____

_____

_____

_____

_____

Amen

A fool vents all his feelings, but a wise man holds them back.
Proverbs 29:11

You, O God, are both tender and kind,
not easily angered, immense in love.
Psalm 86:15 MSG

Daily prayer for help . . .
when I'm battling an addiction

Jesus said, "The Spirit of the Lord is upon Me, because He has anointed Me . . . to proclaim liberty to the captives."

Luke 4:18

Dear Heavenly Father,

I just heard the song "My Deliverer" on the car radio, and I was so overcome by emotion that I had to pull over. Oh, Lord, my wife is right. I can't control this problem anymore. I'm addicted. I'm trapped. My only chance is for You to rescue me. I never thought I'd admit this, but I need a Savior. Please come.

I feel so weak, and the recovery process seems like such a long journey. But my family needs me. Will You walk with me? I know You are strong. You may have to carry me at times, Lord, because I don't know if I can make it. But knowing You will be there gives me hope.

Amen.

God brings out those who are bound into prosperity.
Psalm 68:6

MY PERSONAL PRAYER

Christianity promises to make men free; it never promises to make them independent.

William Ralph Inge

Dear Father:

_____

_____

_____

_____

_____

_____

Amen

The Lord brought them out of darkness and the shadow of death, and broke their chains in pieces.
Psalm 107:14

The Lord gives freedom to the prisoners.
Psalm 146:7

$\mathcal{D}$aily prayer for help . . .
when I'm struggling to let go of the past

*Your sins are forgiven you
for His name's sake.*

1 John 2:12

Dear Heavenly Father,

A thought struck me today: What kind of husband and father would I be if I could drop all the baggage I've been carrying around and leave it all behind? It seems so liberating!

Is it really possible to do that, Lord? My first reaction was that I'd lose my self-identity. My next reaction was, *What about justice?* Do I just let the people who wronged me off the hook? Will You just let me off the hook?

I can't get this concept out of my head, Father. It seems so appealing. I've been a Christian for some time, but maybe I haven't completely understood what forgiveness and grace really mean. Please teach me. And help me to let go.

Amen.

*As far as the east is from the west,
so far has He removed our transgressions from us.*

Psalm 103:12

MY PERSONAL PRAYER

In Christ we can move out of our past into a meaningful present and a breathtaking future.

Erwin W. Lutzer

Dear Father:

_____

_____

_____

_____

_____

_____

Amen

If anyone is in Christ, he is a new creation.
2 Corinthians 5:17

Forgetting those things which are behind and reaching forward to those things which are ahead, I press toward the goal for the prize of the upward call of God in Christ Jesus.
Philippians 3:13–14

I know not the way God leads me,
but well do I know my Guide.

Martin Luther

Daily Prayers for Guidance . . .

Daily prayer for guidance . . .
when I want to know God better

*Jesus said, "He who has seen Me
has seen the Father."*

John 14:9

Dear Heavenly Father,

There is one picture that has stayed on my desk while
the others have come and gone. It's a certain photograph
of my child at age three, and there's just something about
it. Every time I look at it, I long to be the best father I
can be.

I need to know You better, Lord. You're the perfect
Father, and I believe Your promise that You can make
me just like You. I invite Your Spirit to work in my
heart.

Thank You for revealing yourself to me in so many
ways—through Your creation, Your Word, Your Son
Jesus, Your Holy Spirit, and Your church. I pray that
more and more You'll reveal yourself to my child
through me.

Amen.

Everyone who loves is born of God and knows God.
1 John 4:7

MY PERSONAL PRAYER

True knowledge of God will result . . . in our falling on our faces before God in sheer wonder.

John R. W. Stott

Dear Father:

_____

_____

_____

_____

_____

_____

Amen

Jesus said, "No one knows...the Father except the Son, and the one to whom the Son wills to reveal Him."
Matthew 11:27

Everything else is worthless when compared with the priceless gain of knowing Christ Jesus my Lord.
Philippians 3:8 NLT

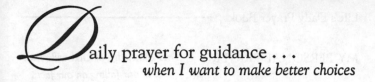

Daily prayer for guidance . . .
when I want to make better choices

*If any of you lacks wisdom,
let him ask of God, who gives to all liberally
and without reproach.*

James 1:5

Dear Heavenly Father,

All day long I face choices as a husband and father. Many come at me with rapid-fire speed, and I must decide quickly. With others I have a little more time to think. But all of them have lasting consequences.

Help me make better choices, Lord. Remind me that at the heart level, even small choices represent very significant decisions: Am I going to be selfish or unselfish? Am I going to be foolish or wise? Am I going to please my own fallen nature, or am I going to please Your Spirit living in me?

I know You will bless my family and me for every good choice I make, large or small. Help me choose well.

Amen.

Your word is a lamp to my feet and a light to my path.
Psalm 119:105

MY PERSONAL PRAYER

*In darkness there is no choice.
It is light that enables us to see the
differences between things; and it is
Christ who gives us light.*

Augustus W. Hare

Dear Father:

_____

_____

_____

_____

_____

_____

Amen

*Whatever a man sows, that he will also reap. . . . He who
sows to the Spirit will of the Spirit reap everlasting life.*
Galatians 6:7–8

To be spiritually minded is life and peace.
Romans 8:6

*D*aily prayer for guidance . . .
when I want to be a good example

Imitate me, just as I also imitate Christ.
1 Corinthians 11:1

Dear Heavenly Father,

I'll never forget hearing my two year old repeat the first adult phrase he'd picked up from me. I asked him if he wanted to go for a ride on his sled, and he replied, "Sounds like a plan!"

It amazes me how much language my kids never needed to be taught; they simply learned it from listening to others. Remind me to always honor You with my speech, Lord. My children are still listening.

They're watching me too, like little hawks. Or maybe little monkeys, the way they imitate everything. Help me remember that my children will continue to emulate my behavior well into adulthood. Help me follow Christ, so I'll be a good example for them—and everyone else who's watching.

Amen.

As for me and my house, we will serve the Lord.
Joshua 24:15

MY PERSONAL PRAYER

If you want your neighbor to see what Christ will do for him, let him see what Christ has done for you.
Henry Ward Beecher

Dear Father:

_____

_____

_____

_____

_____

_____

Amen

Be an example to the believers in word, in conduct, in love, in spirit, in faith, in purity.
1 Timothy 4:12

Show them all this by doing it yourself.
Titus 2:7 MSG

Daily prayer for guidance . . .
when I want to know God's plan

"I know the plans I have for you," says the
Lord. "They are plans for good."
Jeremiah 29:11 NLT

Dear Heavenly Father,

One challenge I've faced as I've grown up, married, and had children is letting go of some dreams. There are things I always wanted to do in my life, but now life seems to get in the way.

In the Bible You reveal yourself as a gardener who prunes fruitful branches so they'll bear more fruit. Help me understand that this is what You are doing with me. Show me which of my dreams are part of Your plan for my life, and which I need to let You prune away.

Help me trust You in this, Father, even though it's a painful process. You are a master gardener, and Your vision for me is far greater than my own.

Amen.

You can make many plans, but the Lord's purpose will prevail.
Proverbs 19:21 NLT

MY PERSONAL PRAYER   *Destiny waits in the hand of God.*
                                          T. S. Eliot

Dear Father:

_____

_____

_____

_____

_____

_____

_____

                                          Amen

Be transformed by the renewing of your mind,
that you may prove what is that good and acceptable
and perfect will of God.
Romans 12:2

"No mind has imagined what God has prepared for those who
love him." But ... God has revealed them to us by his Spirit.
1 Corinthians 2:9–10 NLT

Prayers to Encourage and Comfort the Soul

*D*aily prayer for guidance . . .
when I want to show more love

*Let us continue to love each other since love
comes from God.*

1 John 4:7 MSG

Dear Heavenly Father,

You have been teaching me about love for a long time.
When I got married, I learned that love requires
communication and a lot of give and take. When I
became a parent, I learned about self-sacrifice and
unconditional love.

You've taught me that loving means choosing to let
Your love flow through me.

Continue to teach me about love. I need to learn more
about showing my children love even when I have to
discipline them. I need to learn more about showing my
wife love even when we're arguing about an important issue.

Help me remember that the Bible says You are love.
Remind me that whenever I show love to anyone, I'm
showing them the face of God.

Amen.

*Owe no one anything except to love one another,
for he who loves another has fulfilled the law.*

Romans 13:8

MY PERSONAL PRAYER

Christian love, either towards
God or towards man, is an affair
of the will.

C. S. Lewis

Dear Father:

_____

_____

_____

_____

_____

_____

Amen

The fruit of the Spirit is love.
Galatians 5:22

Jesus said, "This is My commandment,
that you love one another as I have loved you."
John 15:12

Daily prayer for guidance . . .
when I want to walk in integrity

Show me Your ways, O Lord;
teach me Your paths.

Psalm 25:4

Dear Heavenly Father,

I know integrity is a matter of faith. If I trust You to satisfy all my needs, there's no need to be dishonest. Why steal a nickel when the Creator of the universe provides me with everything?

Still, it's tempting sometimes to cut corners here and there, or be less than honest on expense reports or income tax forms. It's incredible how appealing those shiny little nickels can be at times!

Give me wisdom, Lord. Remind me I have nothing to gain by being dishonest. Help me to always walk in Your ways, staying committed to Your perfect standards of integrity. I want to honor You by being a man of honor, and by setting a good example for my children.

Amen.

The path of the just is like the shining sun,
that shines ever brighter unto the perfect day.

Proverbs 4:18

MY PERSONAL PRAYER

*Jesus Christ is not teaching
ordinary integrity, but
supernormal integrity, a likeness
to our Father in heaven.*

Oswald Chambers

Dear Father:

_____

_____

_____

_____

_____

_____

Amen

*The Sovereign Lord is my strength! He will make me as
surefooted as a deer and bring me safely over the mountains.*
Habbakuk 3:19 NLT

He who walks with integrity walks securely.
Proverbs 10:9

$\mathcal{D}$aily prayer for guidance . . .
when I want to give cheerfully

*He who sows bountifully will also
reap bountifully.*

2 Corinthians 9:6

Dear Heavenly Father,

Some people have the spiritual gift of giving. For them, giving is a joy. My wife is so generous that sometimes I think she'd give away our house if You asked her to.

For me, giving is a little harder. It doesn't immediately warm my heart the way it does hers. I have to think it through. Remind me that giving is an act of obedience and faith. Help me remember that our giving supports Your work throughout the world. And remind me about all the blessings You promise for those who give faithfully. I want my family to reap those rewards.

I agree that giving is good, Lord. I just need a little help being more cheerful about doing it.

Amen.

*Honor the Lord with your possessions, and with the firstfruits of
all your increase; so your barns will be filled with plenty.*

Proverbs 3:9–10

MY PERSONAL PRAYER

God has given us two hands—
one for receiving and the other
for giving.

Billy Graham

Dear Father:

_____

_____

_____

_____

_____

_____

_____

Amen

Jesus said, "Give, and it will be given to you: good measure,
pressed down, shaken together, and running over."
Luke 6:38

God loves a cheerful giver.
2 Corinthians 9:7

*D*aily prayer for guidance . . .
when I want to make a wise decision

The testimony of the Lord is sure,
making wise the simple.

Psalm 19:7

Dear Heavenly Father,

I have to make a big decision, and I've done all I can to make it wisely. I've been praying about it, listening for Your voice. I've been reading Your Word, looking for guidance in its truths. I've sought the counsel of wise, trusted Christians. And I've talked things over with my wife to get her perspective.

Now it's time for me to decide, Lord, so speak to me clearly. More than anything, I want Your will for my family. I trust Your wisdom above my own. Only You know the full impact this decision will have on our lives. Yet I know You will lead us to a place of blessing far beyond what we could ever imagine.

Amen.

The Lord gives wisdom; from His mouth come
knowledge and understanding.
Proverbs 2:6

MY PERSONAL PRAYER

The intellect of the wise is like glass; it admits the light of heaven and reflects it.

Augustus John Cuthbert Hare

Dear Father:

_____

_____

_____

_____

_____

Amen

Trust in the Lord with all your heart,
and lean not on your own understanding.
Proverbs 3:5

Through wisdom a house is built, and by understanding it
is established; by knowledge the rooms are filled with all
precious and pleasant riches.
Proverbs 24:3–4

$\mathcal{D}$aily prayer for guidance . . .
when I want God's perspective

> God says, "As the heavens are higher than the
> earth, so are My ways higher than your ways,
> and My thoughts than your thoughts."
>
> Isaiah 55:9

Dear Heavenly Father,

Some friends of ours came to my wife and me for
advice. They've noticed how our faith has strengthened
our relationship, and they want help for their marriage.

As the two of them shared their struggle with us, we
didn't know what to say. Relationship issues can be so
complicated! It's tough to figure out what the real
problem is. Both of them blame each other.

We don't want to take this responsibility lightly, Lord.
So give us Your perspective as we try to help them deal
with their situation. Only You can see their hearts and
understand everything that's going on between them.
Help us see this issue from Your point of view, so we can
offer them godly counsel.

Amen.

Great is our Lord, and mighty in power; His understanding is infinite.
Psalm 147:5

MY PERSONAL PRAYER

What can escape the eye of God,
all seeing,
Or deceive his heart, omniscient?
John Milton

Dear Father:

_____

_____

_____

_____

_____

_____

Amen

The foolishness of God is wiser than men.
1 Corinthians 1:25

There is no creature hidden from His sight, but all things
are naked and open to the eyes of Him.
Hebrews 4:13

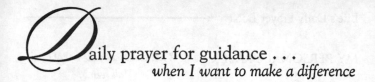

Daily prayer for guidance . . .
when I want to make a difference

*Jesus said, "By this all will know that you are
My disciples, if you have love for one another."*
John 13:35

Dear Heavenly Father,

When it's all said and done, I want my life to have
mattered. I want my time on earth to have been fruitful.
I want to hear You say, "Well done, good and faithful
servant."

I know love is the key to a significant life. So fill my
heart with love, for You, my wife, my children, and all
people. The Bible says that if I love You with all my
heart, and love others as myself, I'll fulfill all Your
commandments.

Lord Jesus, I want everyone to know that I'm Your
disciple. Not just because I tell them so, but because
they see it in my actions, and feel Your love flowing
through me. What a difference that would make!

Amen.

*They will see your honorable behavior,
and they will believe and give honor to God.*
1 Peter 2:12 NLT

MY PERSONAL PRAYER

The way from God to a human heart is through a human heart.
Samuel Dickey Gordon

Dear Father:

_____

_____

_____

_____

_____

_____

Amen

Be ready to speak up and tell anyone who asks why you're living the way you are.
1 Peter 3:15 MSG

Jesus said, "Let your light so shine before men, that they may see your good works and glorify your Father in heaven."
Matthew 5:16

*D*aily prayer for guidance . . .
when I've failed

> *Have mercy upon me, O God, according
> to Your lovingkindness; according to the
> multitude of Your tender mercies, blot out my
> transgressions.*
>
> Psalm 51:1

Dear Heavenly Father,

I blew it again. Please forgive me. I'm not sure how it happened; help me figure it out so it won't happen again. Show me where I went wrong, the little choice I made that snowballed into this big mistake. Next time I want to be wiser, for my sake and for my family's sake.

I feel guilty, Lord, like I need to do something to make up for my failure, to make things right with You. I almost feel like I shouldn't be praying to You now, but should do some kind of penance first.

Yet I know that's wrong. Your Word tells me to come to You just as I am and receive forgiveness. Thank You for Your grace.

Amen.

When I fall, I will arise; when I sit in darkness, the Lord will be a light to me.
Micah 7:8

MY PERSONAL PRAYER

*Failure is an invitation to have
recourse to God.*
Antonin Dalmace Sertillanges

Dear Father:

_____

_____

_____

_____

_____

_____

_____

Amen

*Confess your trespasses to one another, and pray for one
another, that you may be healed.*
James 5:16

*Purge me with hyssop, and I shall be clean; wash me,
and I shall be whiter than snow.*
Psalm 51:7

The pulse of prayer is praise. The heart of prayer is gratitude. The voice of prayer is obedience. The arm of prayer is service.

William Arthur Ward

Daily Prayers of Praise . . .

*D*aily prayer of praise for . . .
life

> *The Lord God formed man of the dust of the ground, and breathed into his nostrils the breath of life.*
>
> Genesis 2:7

Dear Heavenly Father,

What a gift life is! Everything I've ever enjoyed—every sight, sound, taste, smell, and sensation—came to me because You created me. Every pleasant memory, every time of happiness, each moment of laughter is part of Your wonderful gift. Thank You for all that my life has meant to me.

And thank You for making me part of the grand story You are weaving through human history. It still amazes me that when I first started reading the Bible, I felt like an outsider looking in. Now I realize that I'm part of it all!

As I look at my children, I marvel at how You continue to create life, and proceed to write Your story. I give all my praise to You.

Amen.

> *God said: "Before I shaped you in the womb, I knew all about you. Before you saw the light of day, I had holy plans for you."*
>
> Jeremiah 1:5 MSG

MY PERSONAL PRAYER

The Engineer of the universe has made me part of his whole design.
Leigh Nygard

Dear Father:

_____

_____

_____

_____

_____

_____

Amen

Every day of my life was recorded in your book. Every moment was laid out before a single day had passed.
Psalm 139:16 NLT

[God] chose us in [Christ] before the foundation of the world.
Ephesians 1:4

Daily prayer of praise for . . .
God's provision

> God ... *gave us rain from heaven and fruitful seasons, filling our hearts with food and gladness.*
>
> Acts 14:17

Dear Heavenly Father,

You provide for my family so well. When I look back over the years, I see how faithfully You have met our needs in the past, and when I look around now, I see How faithfully You are meeting our needs today. I know I can trust You to provide for us always.

Our needs in the future will be great. We'll have to replace both cars eventually, and we don't want to accumulate more debt. We're trying to eliminate as much debt as possible, because soon the kids will need money for college. I'm glad we have You to rely on. You give us wisdom to work toward our goals, and provide for our needs in ways only You can.

Amen.

> God ... *gives us richly all things to enjoy.*
> 1 Timothy 6:17

MY PERSONAL PRAYER

*In God's faithfulness
lies eternal security.*

Corrie ten Boom

Dear Father:

_____

_____

_____

_____

_____

_____

_____

Amen

*I have not seen the righteous forsaken,
nor his descendants begging bread.*
Psalm 37:25

*[God's] divine power has given to us all things
that pertain to life and godliness.*
2 Peter 1:3

*D*aily prayer of praise for . . .
God's creation

> *God saw everything that He had made,*
> *and indeed it was very good.*
>
> Genesis 1:31

Dear Heavenly Father,

What a beautiful world You created! It's a wonderful place to live, and every day it reflects Your glory. Thank You for this marvelous planet You've given us. Help us to respect it and care for it in a way that's pleasing to You.

It's remarkable to me how a mere photograph of a mountain scene inspires me with praise for Your majesty. And it's just a mere snapshot of Your splendor. What an awesome God You must be!

Help me always to see You in the world around me. Thank You for my wife, with whom I love to share the joy of Your creation. Help us to teach our children to see You everywhere they look.

Amen.

> *The heavens tell of the glory of God.*
> *The skies display his marvelous craftsmanship.*
>
> Psalm 19:1 NLT

MY PERSONAL PRAYER

The sky is the daily bread
of the eyes.
Ralph Waldo Emerson

Dear Father:

_____

_____

_____

_____

_____

_____

Amen

O Lord, what a variety of things you have made!
In wisdom you have made them all.
Psalm 104:24 NLT

May you be blessed by the Lord,
who made heaven and earth.
Psalm 115:15

$\mathcal{D}$aily prayer of praise for . . .
good health

> *Fear the Lord and depart from evil.*
> *It will be health to your flesh, and strength*
> *to your bones.*
>
> Proverbs 3:7–8

Dear Heavenly Father,

I hate to admit it, but I'm getting older. It's been a great life so far. Thank You for the good health You've blessed me with over the years. I've been sick at times, and I've been benched by an injury once or twice, but overall I've been well.

I want to be around for a long time to enjoy my family and be there for them. So help me take care of myself by eating right, getting plenty of sleep, and exercising. Keep me motivated to exercise the spiritual disciplines as well; I know that's good for my body and my soul.

Amen.

He shall be like a tree planted by the rivers of water, that brings forth its
fruit in its season, whose leaf also shall not wither.
Psalm 1:3

MY PERSONAL PRAYER

Health and cheerfulness mutually beget each other.
Joseph Addison

Dear Father:

_____

_____

_____

_____

_____

_____

Amen

A sound mind makes for a robust body.
Proverbs 14:30 MSG

A cheerful heart is good medicine.
Proverbs 17:22 NLT

*D*aily prayer of praise for . . .

those I love

If we walk in the light as He is in the light,
we have fellowship with one another.

1 John 1:7

Dear Heavenly Father,

I praise You for the joy in my house today. On our wedding day, my wife and I committed our marriage to You. As our children were born, we placed their lives in Your hands. We believed Your promise that You would bless us if we made You Lord of our home, and You have been faithful. Thank You, God.

Help us remain faithful to our promise too. In our family, You've created a little body of believers, a small example of Your church. Remind us of that as we read all the "one another" commands in Your Word. Enable us to put them into practice each day. If we do, I know You'll continue to bless our relationships with joy.

Amen.

Be patient with each other, making allowance for
each other's faults because of your love.

Ephesians 4:2 NLT

MY PERSONAL PRAYER

*A happy family is but
an earlier heaven.*

Sir John Bowring

Dear Father:

Amen

Encourage each other and build each other up.
1 Thessalonians 5:11 NLT

Love one another deeply from the heart.
1 Peter 1:22 NRSV

$\mathscr{D}$aily prayer of praise for . . .
how God created me

> *You made all the delicate, inner parts*
> *of my body and knit me together in my*
> *mother's womb.*
>
> Psalm 139:13 NLT

Dear Heavenly Father,

Seeing my children born and watching them grow has given me a new appreciation for the miracle of the human body. It's an incredible piece of engineering and a beautiful work of art. Nobody will ever convince me that such an intricate, well-designed body could ever have been formed by chance. Only You could have created it.

You deserve my praise just for making my physical body, which is only temporary—how much more should I worship You for creating my eternal soul! The wonder of the human spirit is beyond my comprehension.

Help me teach my children how special they are. I want them to understand how valuable they are in Your sight, and in mine.

Amen.

God created man in His own image.
Genesis 1:27

MY PERSONAL PRAYER

God created man because God loves and wanted an object to love. He created man so that he could return his love.

Billy Graham

Dear Father:

_____

_____

_____

_____

_____

_____

Amen

I will praise You, for I am fearfully and wonderfully made.
Psalm 139:14

Bless the Lord, O my soul; and all that is within me, bless His holy name!
Psalm 103:1

$\mathcal{D}$aily prayer of praise for . . .
unexpected blessings

> *[God's] compassions fail not. They are new*
> *every morning; great is Your faithfulness.*
> Lamentations 3:22–23

Dear Heavenly Father,

I should know by now to expect the unexpected with You. I think I must always work hard and pray for good things to happen in my life, and then You surprise me with wonderful blessings out of the blue.

Thank You for all these gifts of grace—for money and items my family receives for no reason. For times when You thwart our busy agenda and leave us no choice but to relax and enjoy one another. For times when we feel like the rich and famous for a while because others allow us to enjoy their blessings.

I especially praise You for surprising us as we grow spiritually. How delightful it is every time You reveal more of yourself!

Amen.

> *You give them drink from the river of Your pleasures.*
> Psalm 36:8

MY PERSONAL PRAYER

God particularly pours out his blessings upon those who know how much they need him.

Robert Harold Schuller

Dear Father:

_____

_____

_____

_____

_____

_____

Amen

Surely goodness and mercy shall follow me all the days of my life.
Psalm 23:6

[God] has blessed us with every spiritual blessing in the heavenly places in Christ.
Ephesians 1:3

_D_aily prayer of praise for . . .
love

The Lord has appeared of old to me,
saying: "Yes, I have loved you with an
everlasting love."

Jeremiah 31:3

Dear Heavenly Father,

You are worthy of all my praise, because above everything You are a God of love. Of all Your excellent qualities, I'm most thankful for this. You are the source of love, and I love You in return.

Knowing that You love me makes me feel valuable, fills my life with meaning, and gives me hope. It helps me trust You and provides me with a sense of safety and security. Your love makes me want to do great things for You, gives me confidence to try, and empowers me to succeed.

Your love inspires me to love the people around me. Help me teach my children about its incredible richness and depth, and let it flow through my own heart to them.

Amen.

You shall love the Lord your God with all your heart,
with all your soul, and with all your strength.
Deuteronomy 6:5

MY PERSONAL PRAYER

*Some day . . . we shall harness
for God the energies of love,
and then, for the second time in
the history of the world, man will
have discovered fire.*

Pierre Teilhard de Chardin

Dear Father:

_____

_____

_____

_____

_____

_____

Amen

*The commandments ... are all summed up in this saying,
namely, "You shall love your neighbor as yourself."*
Romans 13:9

What is important is faith expressing itself in love.
Galatians 5:6 NLT

*D*aily prayer of praise for . . .
eternal life

> *Jesus said, "I have come that they may*
> *have life, and that they may have it more*
> *abundantly."*
>
> John 10:10

Dear Heavenly Father,

The greatest blessing You have given me is knowing that my relationship with You will last for all eternity.

That knowledge colors every aspect of my life with joy. And the more I grow spiritually, the more You've shown me that the gift of eternity is in my hands right now. I don't have to wait for heaven to start experiencing it; my eternal life with You has already begun! Jesus said that whoever trusts in Him will never die, and I believe Him.

I know it's all true, because You have already blessed me with the abundant life He promised. My life with You is full. I don't ever want it to end—and I'm so thankful it never will!

Amen.

[Jesus] died for us so that we can live with him forever.
1 Thessalonians 5:10 NLT

MY PERSONAL PRAYER

*When ten thousand times ten
thousand times ten thousand years
have passed, eternity will
have just begun.*

Dear Father:

Billy Sunday

_____

_____

_____

_____

_____

_____

Amen

*God, who is rich in mercy . . .
made us alive together with Christ.*
Ephesians 2:4–5

*God so loved the world that He gave His only begotten Son,
that whoever believes in Him should not perish but
have everlasting life.*
John 3:16

$\mathcal{D}$aily prayer of praise for . . .

the Bible

Forever, O Lord, Your word is settled
in heaven.

Psalm 119:89

Dear Heavenly Father,

Thank You for giving us the Bible. What a rich source of wisdom and inspiration! Every time I open it, I learn more about You, more about others, and more about myself. Long ago I started plumbing the depths of Your Word, and I know I've only just begun.

As I grow spiritually, I keep discovering deeper levels of meaning in the Scriptures. Each time I experience the Bible's truths in my life, I want to read it all over again so I can understand it more fully. I know the Bible can help me be a better person, a better man, and a better father.

Keep opening my mind to scriptural truths, Lord. Keep opening my heart to accept them.

Amen.

The law of the Lord is perfect, reviving the soul.
Psalm 19:7 NLT

MY PERSONAL PRAYER

The Bible is alive, it speaks to me;
it has feet, it runs after me; it has
hands, it lays hold on me.

Martin Luther

Dear Father:

_____

_____

_____

_____

_____

_____

Amen

Oh, how I love all you've revealed;
I reverently ponder it all the day long.
Psalm 119:97 MSG

I hope in Your word.
Psalm 119:147

Daily prayer of praise for . . .

heaven

> Jesus said, "There are many rooms in my
> Father's home, and I am going to prepare a
> place for you."
>
> John 14:2 NLT

Dear Heavenly Father,

I can almost see a twinkle in Your eye whenever I read
1 Corinthians 2:9. I can almost hear the laughter in
Your voice as You say, "You have no idea what I have in
store for you!"

This verse comes to mind whenever I think about
heaven. I love it because it blows away any image of a
ho-hum afterlife with nothing to do but sit on a cloud.
My imagination starts working overtime, knowing there
are no boundaries to the possibilities of paradise.

I praise You for the promise of heaven. Thank You for
revealing just enough about it to set our hopes soaring.
Show me how to plant that seed of hope in my children.

Amen.

We are receiving a kingdom which cannot be shaken.
Hebrews 12:28

MY PERSONAL PRAYER

Heaven is the perfectly ordered and
harmonious enjoyment of God and
of one another in God.

Saint Augustine

Dear Father:

_____

_____

_____

_____

_____

_____

_____

Amen

God has reserved a priceless inheritance for his children.
It is kept in heaven for you.
1 Peter 1:4 NLT

The home of God is now among his people!
He will live with them, and they will be his people.
Revelation 21:3 NLT

Topical Index

The chief purpose of prayer is that
God may be glorified in the answer.

R. A. Torrey

For additions, deletions, corrections,
or clarifications in future editions of this text,
please contact Paul Shepherd, Editor in Chief
for Elm Hill Books.
Email pshepherd@elmhillbooks.com.

Products from Elm Hill Books may be purchased in
bulk for educational, business, fundraising, or sales
promotional use. For information, please email
SpecialMarkets@ThomasNelson.com.

Additional copies of this book and other
titles from ELM HILL BOOKS are available from
your local bookstore.

Other titles in this series:

Life's Daily Prayer Book
Life's Daily Prayer Book for Teachers
Life's Daily Prayer Book for Women
Life's Daily Prayer Book for Graduates
Life's Daily Prayer Book for Mothers